INSIDE HISTORY

Pirate Ship

Illustrated by Peter Dennis

W
FRANKLIN WATTS
LONDON•SYDNEY

Contents

The Golden Age of Piracy

Pirates, or sea robbers, have been around for thousands of years. Greek pirates terrorised cargo ships in the Mediterranean Sea over 4,000 years ago, and piracy still goes on in some parts of the world today. But between the 16th and 18th centuries piracy became very common, particularly in the Spanish Main – the Caribbean coast of South America. This period is sometimes called the Golden Age of Piracy.

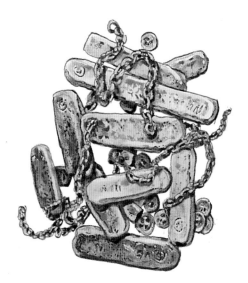

At this time, Europeans had only recently discovered South and Central America. Spanish explorers claimed a lot of these new lands, rich in gold and silver, for Spain. They sent this treasure back to their home country in large, heavily armed sailing ships called galleons. Such treasure ships were irresistible to pirates. They attacked them and stole the riches they contained.

Why were so many sailors prepared to become pirates? Life on board ship in those days was very harsh. Many sailors of navy or merchant ships had been kidnapped or tricked into going to sea. A life of piracy offered them freedom and the chance to get rich, so perhaps it is not surprising that many sailors deserted or mutinied against their captains and became pirates.

The Jolly Roger: the pirate flag

Gunwales: the top-deck rail

The poop deck: an open raised deck at the stern

The rear end of the ship is called the stern.

THE CAPTAIN

Some pirate captains rule their crew by fear and cruelty, but most are only in charge by agreement with their men. If they become unpopular, or treat the crew badly, the pirates will happily remove them, and appoint someone else as their leader instead. The captain usually shares his duties with his second-in-command, the quartermaster.

Swivel gun

Musketoon

Cutlass

Window of the captain's Great Cabin

Preparing to fire a small cannon at the enemy

STEERING THE SHIP

The helmsman steers the ship from the gun deck using wooden rods, called the tiller and the whipstaff, to move the rudder. The rudder is a huge wooden paddle at the stern. On some ships the rudder is controlled by a wheel on the main deck instead of a whipstaff.

Rudder

SHIP'S GUNS

The pirate ship has several cannon. These are simple guns mounted on a wheeled carriage. This makes them easy to roll back for loading with gunpowder and shot. This ship also has swivel guns mounted on the gunwales. These can be turned from side to side to aim.

The pirate crew show off their weapons.

Mainsail

Ratlines

Main mast

Rigging

Sailors usually go barefoot to help prevent them slipping on wet wooden decks.

RIGGING AND RATLINES

The rigging is the ropes and chains that support and control the masts, yards and sails. Ratlines are the rope ladders fixed to the rigging. Sailors use these to climb up to the sails. Men hanging from the ratlines can also attack invaders on the deck below with their guns and cutlasses.

CAPTAIN'S QUARTERS

The captain has use of the Great Cabin, the largest room on the ship. This is where he entertains guests. The Great Cabin also serves both as a dining room for the captain and his senior crew members, and as a map room, where the captain can spread out navigational charts on the large table. Next door a crewman is tidying the captain's bedchamber.

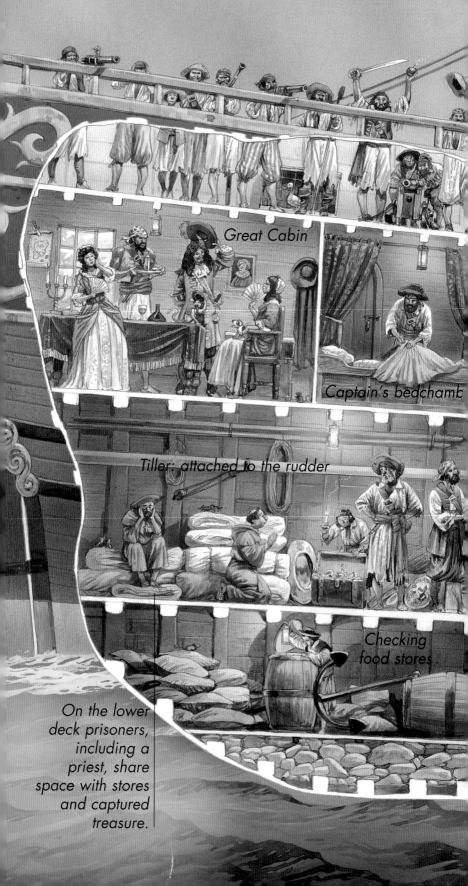

Great Cabin

Captain's bedchamb

Tiller: attached to the rudder

Checking food stores

On the lower deck prisoners, including a priest, share space with stores and captured treasure.

The ship's stern

Welcome aboard! This pirate ship is a brigantine, a fast, medium-sized ship favoured by pirates. It was captured by its lawless crew in the Caribbean Sea. Not only are they fast, but brigantines can also sail into shallow waters where heavier warships cannot follow. The stern, or rear, of the ship, has four decks and houses the captain's quarters and some of the stores. The Jolly Roger is flown from the stern. Each pirate captain has his own flag design, but skulls and cutlasses are always popular subjects.

Manning the whipstaff

Gunpowder stores

Pumping out the bilges

Water stored in barrels

Heavy rocks provide ballast in the bilges to help stabilise the ship.

Bilges

Dolphins love to swim along the side of the ship. They entertain the sailors with their spectacular leaps.

The ship's bow

Here at the bow is the fo'c'sle (short for forecastle), or front deck. This is often higher than the rest of the top deck to give a good view. Most of the crew have their sleeping quarters here at the front of the ship. Below deck is the ship's kitchen, or galley, reached from above by stairs called a companionway.

THE CREW

This crew is made up of hardened sailors who have turned to a life of piracy. They have far more freedom as pirates than as normal sailors, and are treated much better. There are many more men on board than are needed to crew the ship. The extra men will be used to crew any ships they capture but, in the meantime, it means they all do less work on board.

Swivel gun

Axe

Using a small sail boat is the quickest way to get to shore.

Rubbish is thrown into the sea.

This pirate is taking a risk if he falls in – most sailors cannot swim!

Cutlass

Pistol

Foremast

MASTS AND SAILS

This ship has two masts. The foremast at the front carries a square sail, while the main mast can have either a triangular or a square sail. Pirates often changed the masts and sails of the ships they captured to make them faster.

Swivel gun

Musket

Open gun-port

Anchor

The anchor is secured to the ship with a strong rope.

NAVIGATION

Finding your way around once you are out of sight of land is no easy task. The captain uses a compass and charts to help him. He can work out how far north or south the ship is from the position of the sun. He uses an instrument called a backstaff to measure the sun's position.

LIFE ON BOARD

It is very dark, damp and cramped below deck. The crew have to share the limited space with animals, food, water and gunpowder stores. With so many people and animals crowded together, it can be extremely noisy and smelly below decks as well.

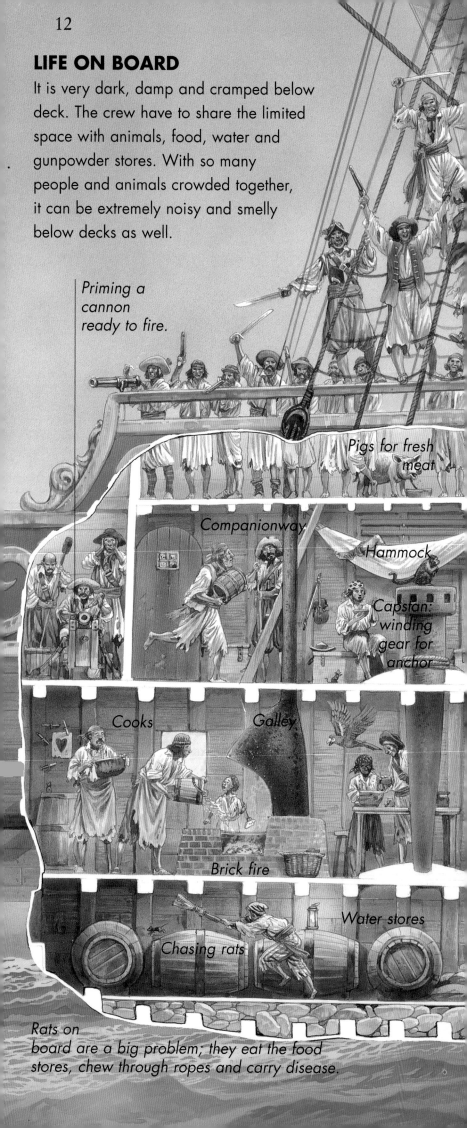

Priming a cannon ready to fire.

Pigs for fresh meat

Companionway

Hammock

Capstan: winding gear for anchor

Cooks

Galley

Brick fire

Chasing rats

Water stores

Rats on board are a big problem; they eat the food stores, chew through ropes and carry disease.

SHIP'S GALLEY

This is where all the cooking is done. After a few days at sea, fresh-food supplies will have run out. From now on it's salted meat, turtle stew and hard ship's biscuits riddled with maggots for breakfast, lunch and dinner!

Square sail

Lookout

Bowsprit with ropes supporting the mast.

Mermaid figurehead: this helps the crew identify their own ship in dock.

The front end of the ship is called the bow.

Cannon ready to fire

Galley stores

Beer barrel

Fresh supplies

Prisoner

Ballast

Pirates leaving the ship in a small boat.

Most sailors sleep in hammocks slung from the low ceilings. These take up less space than bunks or beds.

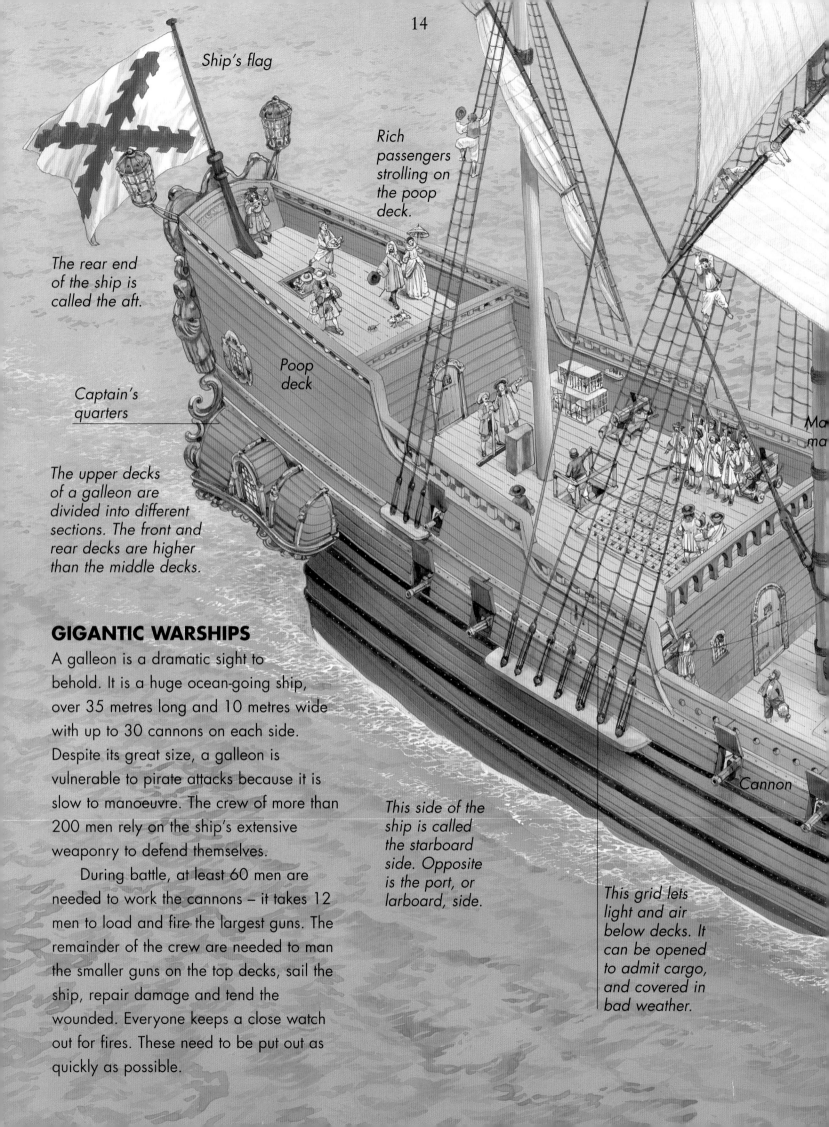

Ship's flag

Rich passengers strolling on the poop deck.

The rear end of the ship is called the aft.

Poop deck

Captain's quarters

The upper decks of a galleon are divided into different sections. The front and rear decks are higher than the middle decks.

Ma ma

Cannon

GIGANTIC WARSHIPS

A galleon is a dramatic sight to behold. It is a huge ocean-going ship, over 35 metres long and 10 metres wide with up to 30 cannons on each side. Despite its great size, a galleon is vulnerable to pirate attacks because it is slow to manoeuvre. The crew of more than 200 men rely on the ship's extensive weaponry to defend themselves.

During battle, at least 60 men are needed to work the cannons – it takes 12 men to load and fire the largest guns. The remainder of the crew are needed to man the smaller guns on the top decks, sail the ship, repair damage and tend the wounded. Everyone keeps a close watch out for fires. These need to be put out as quickly as possible.

This side of the ship is called the starboard side. Opposite is the port, or larboard, side.

This grid lets light and air below decks. It can be opened to admit cargo, and covered in bad weather.

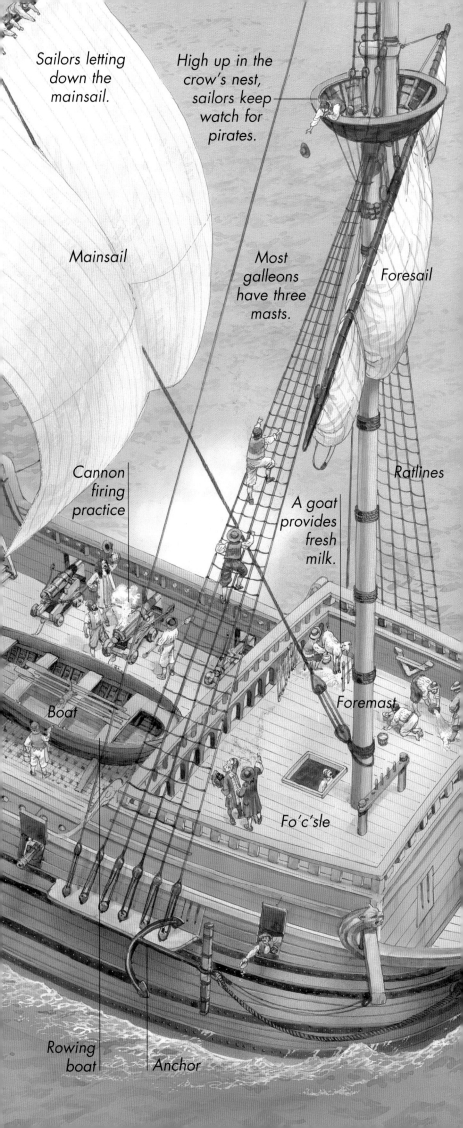

Sailors letting down the mainsail.

High up in the crow's nest, sailors keep watch for pirates.

Mainsail

Most galleons have three masts.

Foresail

Cannon firing practice

A goat provides fresh milk.

Ratlines

Boat

Foremast

Fo'c'sle

Rowing boat

Anchor

Helmsman
steering ship

Captain's
sleeping
quarters

Rats were
a problem
on all
ships.

This brick oven in
the galley protects
the wooden ship
from the hot fire.

Cargo
hold

Water
barrels

Cannonballs

Rock ballast in the
bottom of the ship
stops it tipping over
in high seas.

Spanish galleon

This majestic galleon is on its way back to Spain laden with gold and other treasure from the Americas. The pirates have spotted it coming their way and have decided to try to capture it. This is an ambitious plan. The galleon is large and very well armed, but the pirates have a fearsome reputation. If they are lucky they can negotiate with the Spanish captain to give up without a fight. But the captain is proud and stubborn – and he's in no mood to surrender ...

Crew relaxing

Live parrots

Cargo hold

Capstan

Rope

Figurehead

Bowsprit

Spare sails

Food stores

Ornately carved prow

Gold ingots

GALLEON AHOY!

The pirate ship pulls up alongside the galleon. The pirates use grappling irons to hold the ships together so that their armed men can swarm aboard.

Spanish captain's cabin

Jolly Roger

Sail

Ratlines

Swivel guns

PREPARE TO BOARD!

Normally, a pirate ship would meet little resistance from a galleon. Pirate crews often vastly outnumbered the crew of a merchant vessel, and to save lives, the merchant captain would surrender. But sometimes, as here, the galleon would put up a fight. The pirates use grappling lines to pull the two ships together and swiftly board the galleon.

Moving an injured man below deck.

Slinging grappling irons across the gap,

CUTLASSES

The pirates' preferred sword is the cutlass. Its short, curved blade is easier to wield in the tight spaces on board ship than a longer sword, such as a sabre or rapier.

Main mast

Trying to escape in a small boat

Gunwales

Using the boat as cover during the fighting.

Firing on the enemy.

Mast damaged by cannon fire from the galleon.

Galley
fire

Stores

Gun
deck

Stores

Pirate
surgeon

MUSKETOONS

Musketoons are small muskets fired from the shoulder. They are popular with pirates because their smaller size makes them easier to use on board ship. But even so, they are still slow and awkward as they only fire one shot at a time.

Attack!

After a long chase, the pirate ship has come alongside the galleon. The Spanish ship is not quick enough to get away, but its captain has no intention of giving in. He refuses to parley with the pirates and gives orders to open fire. His cannons soon find their mark, and smash through the pirate ship's foremast.

Spanish captain

Pirate captain

Capstan

Main mast

Fo'c'sle

THE PORT AND GOVERNOR

Some French and English ports in the Caribbean provide pirate ships with a safe haven. The governor here supports the pirates because of the wealth they bring to the town. He can even issue Letters of Marque, authorizing the capture of Spanish merchant vessels.

Some governors take bribes from the pirates, but this has to be done in deadly secret. If they are found out, they will be stripped of their post.

COURTHOUSE AND JAIL

The pirates spend much of their money getting drunk in the town's taverns and bars. But their rowdy antics can land them in jail. Conditions in the jail are primitive and disease is rife. Some unlucky ones may even die before their case is ever heard.

Catholic church

Buildings damaged by cannon fire

Courthouse and jail

Pirate harbour

The raid on the galleon ended in dismal failure. The galleon's gunpowder store was hit by the pirates' cannons. It exploded, and, unfortunately for the pirates, the galleon sank before they were able to retrieve all the treasure. They have come back to port to take on supplies.

A party in the governor's house

Decorating

Soldier on lookout duty

Pirate brigantine

Inside the tavern

Pirates coming ashore

Winching up goods taken from the pirates

TREASURES OF THE SPANISH MAIN

Many ships were lost in the Spanish Main, both to pirates and to violent tropical storms, called hurricanes. Rich cargoes went down with them and lots of people have since searched for the wrecks of these treasure ships. Luckily for the captain's divers the sea is fairly shallow here, so the wreck is not too deep for the divers to reach, and there is enough light from the surface for them to find their way.

DANGEROUS DIVE

People can normally hold their breath underwater for only a minute or so, but pearl and coral divers train themselves to hold their breath for several minutes. Even so, exploring the inside of the wreck like this is very dangerous, but the rewards on offer are so great, the divers are prepared to take the risk.

Turtles

Ratlines

Gunport

Cannonball damage

A diver struggles to the surface with a piece of the treasure.

Stingrays

Jellyfish

Broken spar

Hammerhead
shark

The ship has almost
broken in two here.

Shark

Barrels

Cannon

Treasure
chest

PIECES OF EIGHT

The Spanish made much of the gold and silver they obtained from the Americas into coins. Gold coins were called "doubloons" and silver coins were "pesos". These were divided into eight smaller silver coins called "reals", which had an "8" stamped on them. This led to the term, "pieces of eight" being used for these Spanish silver coins.

Spanish pieces of eight

CORAL

Corals are tiny animals that thrive in warm shallow seas like the Caribbean. They group together in colonies and make hard cases to live in. These build up into fantastically shaped reefs and are often brightly coloured. Lots of other sea creatures, such as fish and crabs, live among the coral.

Food stores

Treasure chests

Coral reef

Shipwreck

It has been almost a year since the galleon sank, but the pirate captain remembers its exact position. He has returned with some divers who will swim down to the wreck and try and recover the treasure.

This hammerhead shark has been making a meal of some of the objects that went down with the Spanish galleon.

Hammock

Turtle

Capstan

Main mast

Crow's nest

Treasure

Glossary

Backstaff A tool that measures the sun's position, and shows how far north or south the ship has travelled.

Ballast Stones packed into the bottom of the ship, or **bilges**, to keep the ship upright, especially in rough weather.

Bilges The lowest part of the ship where ballast is placed. They tend to fill up with smelly, stagnant water.

Brigantine A fast, two-masted ship much favoured by pirates.

Cutlass A pirate sword with a short, broad, sometimes curved blade.

Desertion When a sailor abandons his ship for a better life, often to become a pirate.

Doubloon A Spanish gold coin.

Galleon A large, three-masted cargo ship used mainly by the Spanish to transport treasure back to Spain.

Grappling iron A rope with a many-pronged iron hook on the end used to secure the two ships together.

Gunports Square holes fitted with hinged lids in the side of the ship to shoot cannon balls through.

Jolly Roger The flag flown by pirate ships.

Musket A long, single-shot gun.

Musketoon A shorter version of the **musket**, popular with pirates.

Mutiny When a group of sailors are in open rebellion against their captain.

Parley To speak with an enemy to see if it is possible to avoid a fight.

Pieces of eight The pirate name for Spanish silver coins.

Spanish Main The Caribbean coast of South America, claimed by Spain.